UKULELE

TOP HITS OF 2017

T0077041

ISBN 978-1-5400-0308-9

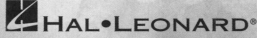

HAL•LEONARD®

7777 W. BLUEMOUND RD. P.O. BOX 13819 MILWAUKEE, WI 53213

Visit Hal Leonard Online at
www.halleonard.com

CONTENTS

Believer

Words and Music by Daniel Reynolds, Wayne Sermon, Ben McKee, Daniel Platzman,
Justin Trantor, Mattias Larsson and Robin Fredricksson

sulk - ing ____ to the mass - es, writ - ing my po - ems ____ for the few that looked at me,

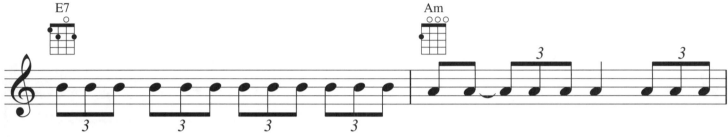

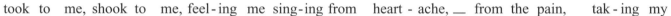

took to me, shook to me, feel-ing me sing-ing from heart - ache, __ from the pain, tak-ing my

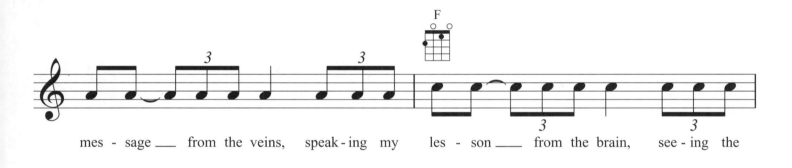

mes - sage __ from the veins, speak-ing my les - son ___ from the brain, see-ing the

𝄋 Chorus

beau - ty ____ through the... pain! You made me a, you made me a be-

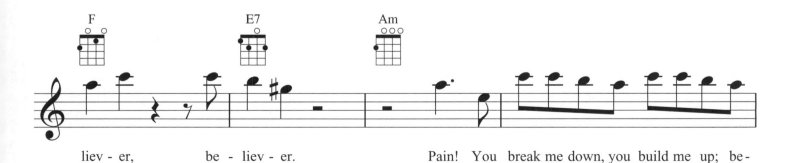

liev - er, be - liev - er. Pain! You break me down, you build me up; be-

liev - er, be - liev - er. Pain! _____ Oh,

let the bul-lets fly, oh, let them rain. _____ My life, my love, my drive, they came from...

N.C. Am F To Coda 1 To Coda 2

pain! You made me a, you made me a be - liev - er, be -

Verse
E7 Am

liev - er. 3. Third things third: send a prayer to the ones ___ up a -

F E7 Am

bove. All the hate that you've heard has turned your spir - it to a dove, oh, ooh, ___

your spir - it up a - bove, oh, ooh. _____ I was

Pre-Chorus

chok - ing ____ in the crowd, liv - ing my brain up ____ in the cloud, fall - ing like

ash - es ____ to the ground, hop - ing my feel - ings, __ they would drown. But they

nev - er did, ev - er lived, ebb - ing and flow - ing, in - hib - it - ed, lim - it - ed, till it broke up and it

D.S. al Coda 1

Coda 1

rained down, it rained __ down __ like... liev - er.

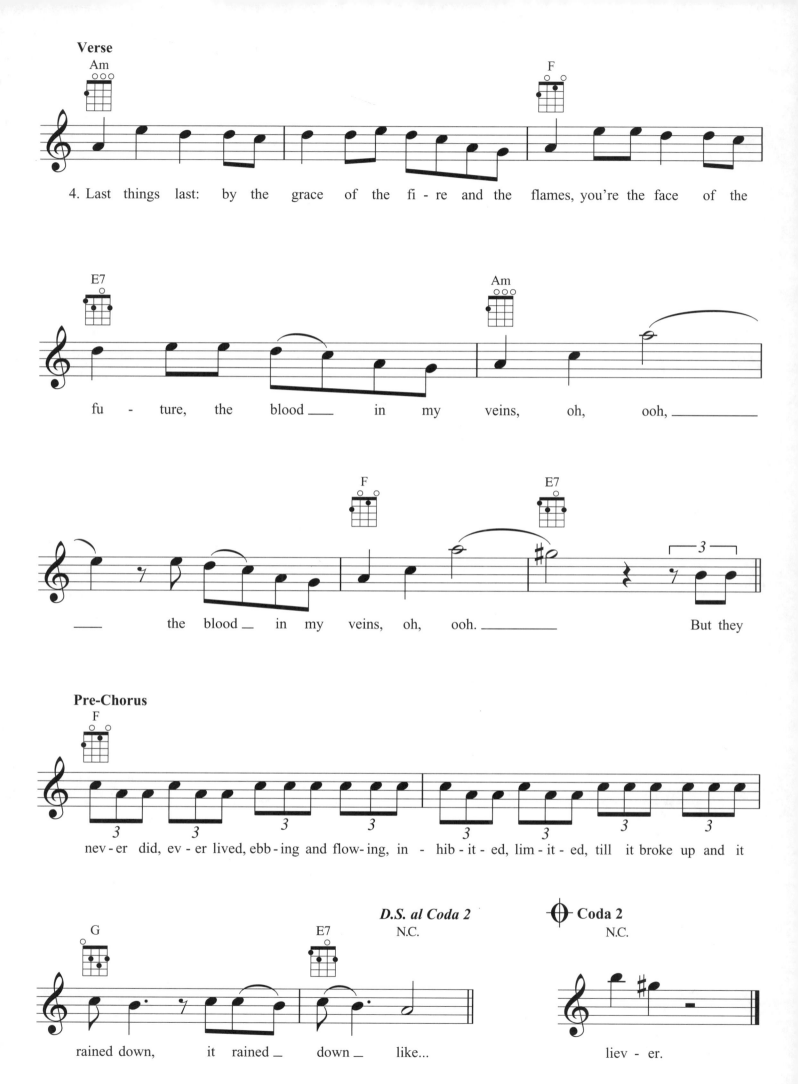

Verse

4. Last things last: by the grace of the fi - re and the flames, you're the face of the

fu - ture, the blood ___ in my veins, oh, ooh, ___

___ the blood ___ in my veins, oh, ooh. ___ But they

Pre-Chorus

nev - er did, ev - er lived, ebb - ing and flow - ing, in - hib - it - ed, lim - it - ed, till it broke up and it

D.S. al Coda 2   **Coda 2**

rained down, it rained ___ down ___ like...   liev - er.

Body Like a Back Road

Words and Music by Sam Hunt, Josh Osborne, Shane McAnally and Zach Crowell

Chained to the Rhythm

Words and Music by Katy Perry, Max Martin, Sia Furler, Ali Payami and Skip Marley

First note

Verse
Moderate Dance Pop

1. Are we cra - zy? Liv - ing our ___ lives through ___

___ a lens. ___ Trapped in our ___ white pick -

- et fence ___ like or - na - ments. ___ So

com - f'ta - ble we're liv - ing in a bub - ble, bub - ble. So

stum - bl - ing a - round like a wast - ed zom - bie. Yeah, we think we're free.

Drink, this one's on me. We're all chained to the rhy - thm,

1.

to the rhy - thm, to the rhy - thm. _____ 3. Are we

2. **Bridge**

to the rhy - thm, to the rhy - thm. _____ It is my de - si - re:

break down the walls to con - nect, in - spi - re. Hey, up in - a your high place, li - ars,

time is tick - ing for the em - pire. The truth they feed is fee - ble as so

man - y times ___ be - fore. ___   They greed o - ver ___ the peo - ple. ____ They

stum - bl - ing and fum - bl - ing and we a - bout to ri - ot. They

D.S. al Coda

Coda

woke up, they woke up the li - ons.   to the rhy - thm, to the rhy - thm.

It goes

Outro

on and on ___ and on. ___   It goes

on and on ___ and on. ___   It goes on and on ___ and on. __

___ 'Cause we're all chained _____ to the rhy - thm.

Castle on the Hill

Words and Music by Ed Sheeran and Benjamin Levin

1. When I was six years old I broke my leg, and I was run-ning from my broth-er and his friends, and tast-ed the sweet per-fume of the moun-tain grass I rolled down. I was young-er then. Take me back to when

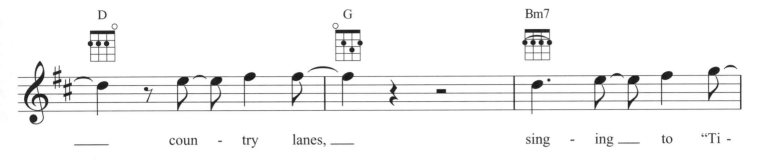

_____ coun - try lanes, _____ sing - ing _____ to "Ti -

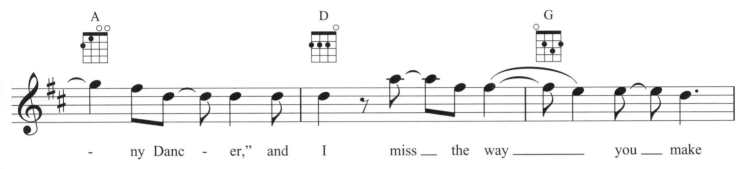

- ny Danc - er," and I miss _____ the way _____ you _____ make

me _____ feel, and it's _____ real, when we watched _____ the sun _____

To Coda ⊕

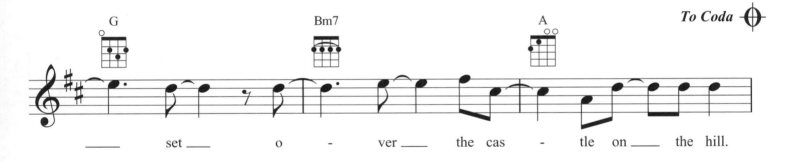

_____ set _____ o - ver _____ the cas - tle on _____ the hill.

Verse

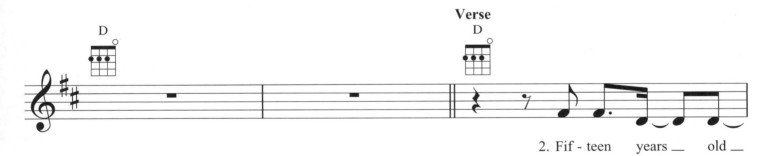

2. Fif - teen years _____ old _____

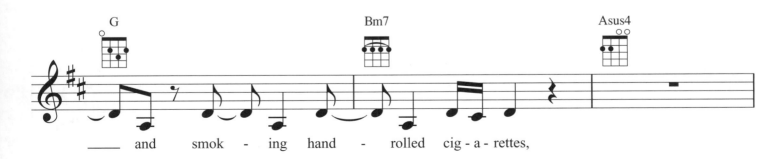

_____ and smok - ing hand - rolled cig - a - rettes,

run - ning from the law _____ through the back fields _ and

get - ting drunk _ with _ my _ friends. Had my _ first kiss _

_ on Fri - day night; ___ I ___ don't reck -

on that I did ___ it _____ right, _ but I was young - er ___ then.

D.S. al Coda

Take _ me back to ___ when ___ we ___ found

Coda

Interlude

8va - - - - - - - - - - -

Hee - hoo, _____ o - ver ___ the cas -

-tle on ___ the hill,   hee - hoo, _____ o-

-ver ___ the cas - tle on ___ the hill.

Bridge

One __ friend left _

____ to sew __ clothes, and   one __ works down ____ by __ the coast;

one had __ two kids ___ but lives a - lone;   one's broth-

-er o - ver - dosed;   one's _ al - read - y on his sec - ond wife;

one's ___ just bare - ly get - ting by. But

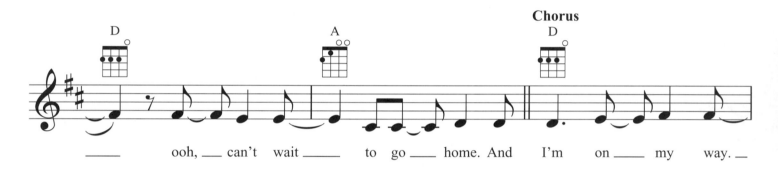

these peo - ple raised ___ me and I, _____

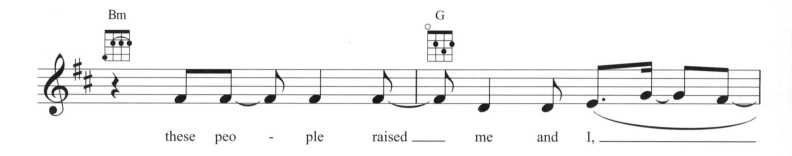

Chorus

___ ooh, ___ can't wait ___ to go ___ home. And I'm on ___ my way. __

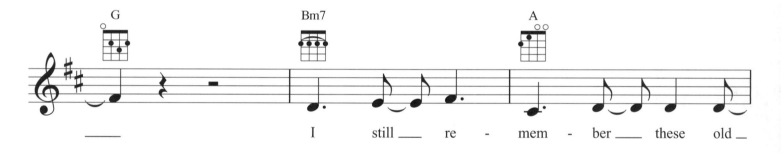

___ I still ___ re - mem - ber ___ these old __

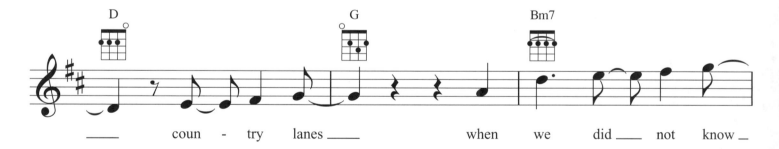

___ coun - try lanes ___ when we did ___ not know __

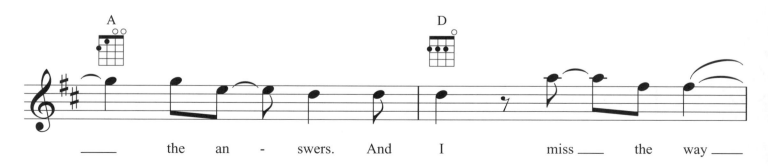

___ the an - swers. And I miss ___ the way __

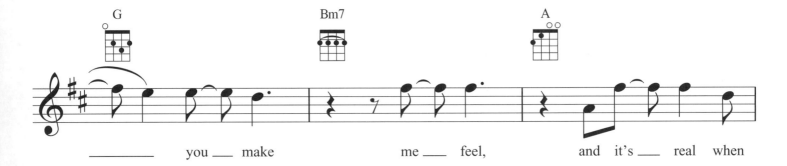

you ___ make ___ me ___ feel, ___ and it's ___ real when

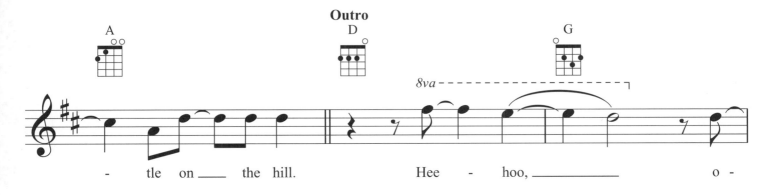

we watched ___ the sun ___ set ___ o - ver ___ the cas -

Outro

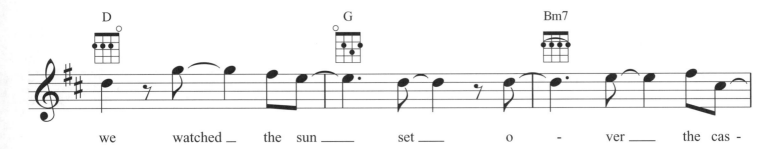

- tle on ___ the hill. Hee - hoo, _____ o-

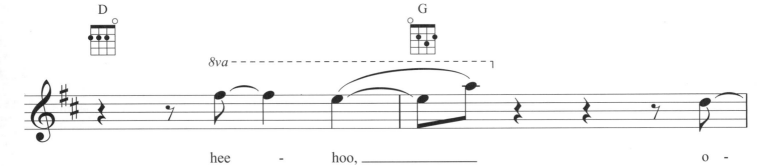

- ver ___ the cas - tle on ___ the hill,

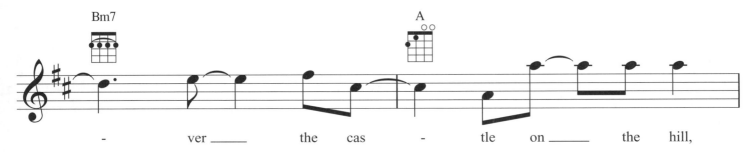

hee - hoo, _____ o-

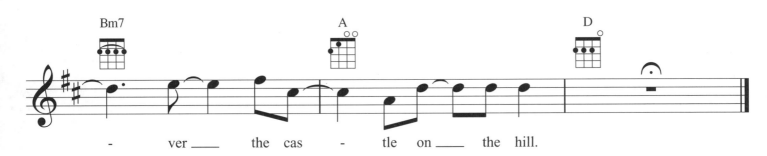

- ver ___ the cas - tle on ___ the hill.

City of Stars

from LA LA LAND

Music by Justin Hurwitz
Lyrics by Benj Pasek & Justin Paul

dreams may fi - n'lly come true.

Verse

2. Cit - y of stars, ___ just one thing ev - 'ry - bod - y wants, ___ there in the bars ___ and through the smoke-screen of the crowd - ed res - tau - rants: ___ ___ it's love. Yes, all we're look - ing for is love from some - one else. _____

Sebastian: A

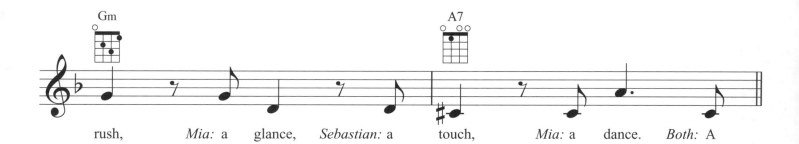

rush, *Mia:* a glance, *Sebastian:* a touch, *Mia:* a dance. *Both:* A

Bridge

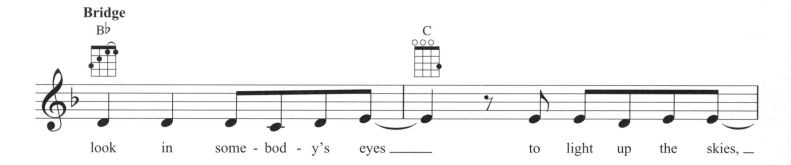

look in some-bod-y's eyes ____ to light up the skies, __

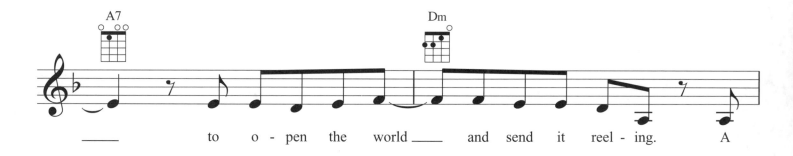

____ to o-pen the world ____ and send it reel-ing. A

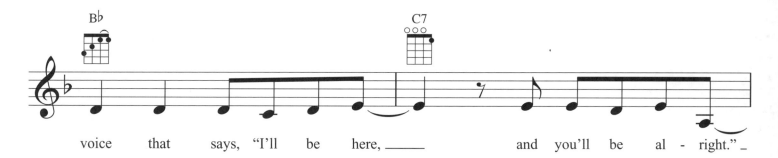

voice that says, "I'll be here, ____ and you'll be al-right." _

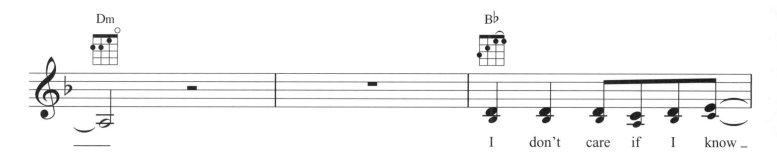

____ I don't care if I know _

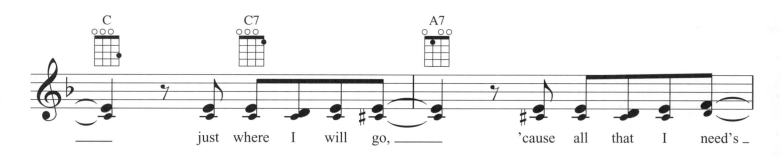

____ just where I will go, ____ 'cause all that I need's _

Despacito

Words and Music by Luis Fonsi, Erika Ender, Justin Bieber,
Jason Boyd, Marty James Garton and Ramón Ayala

feel- in' some kind of way. ____ Make me wan - na sa - vor ev -'ry mo - ment slow -

- ly, slow - ly. _____ You fit me, tail - or -

made love, how you put it on. __ Got the on - ly key, know how to turn it on. __

The way you nib -ble on my ear, the on - ly words I wan - na hear: Ba - by, take it

Pre-Chorus

slow so we can last long. __ Tú, tú e - res el i - mán y yo soy el me -

tal. Me voy a - cer - can - do y voy ar - man - do el plan. Só - lo con pen -

sar - lo se a - ce - ler - a el pul - so.   Oh,   yeah.

Ya,   ya me es - tá   gus - tan - do más de lo nor - mal.   To - dos mis sen -

ti - dos van pi - dien - do más. ___   Es - to hay que to - mar - lo sin nin - gún   a - pu -

%. **Chorus 1**

- ro.   Des - pa - ci - to.   Quie - ro res - pi -

rar tu cue - llo des - pa - ci - to.   De - ja que te   di - ga co - sas al o - í -

- do,   pa - ra que te a - cuer - des si no es - tás   con - mi - go.

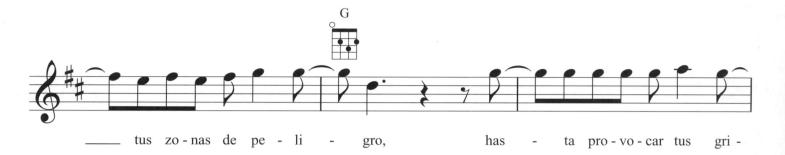

G

_____ tus zo - nas de pe - li - gro, has - ta pro - vo - car tus gri -

D   A   *To Coda*

- tos,   y que ol - vi - des tu a - pe - lli - do.

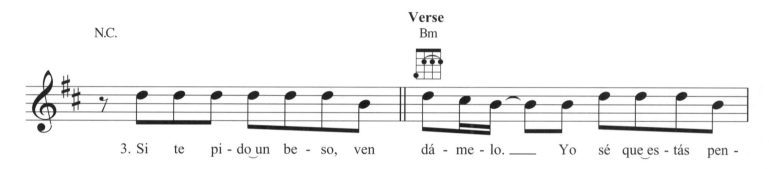

N.C.   **Verse**
                              Bm

3. Si te pi - do un be - so, ven dá - me - lo. _____ Yo sé que es - tás pen -

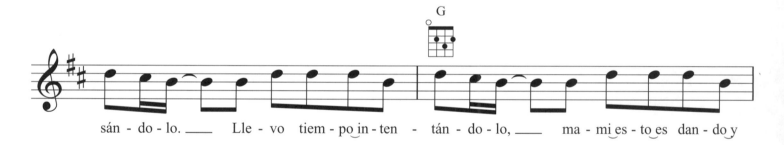

G

sán - do - lo. _____ Lle - vo tiem - po in - ten - tán - do - lo, _____ ma - mi es - to es dan - do y

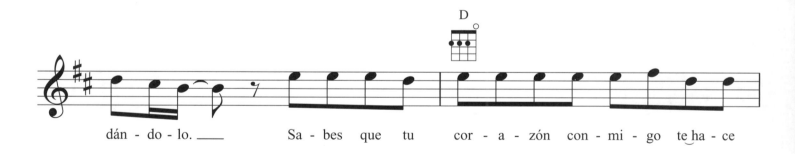

D

dán - do - lo. _____ Sa - bes que tu cor - a - zón con - mi - go te ha - ce

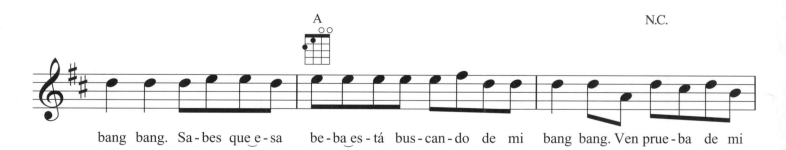

A   N.C.

bang bang. Sa - bes que e - sa be - ba es - tá bus - can - do de mi bang bang. Ven prue - ba de mi

bo - ca pa - ra ver có - mo te sa - be. Quie - ro, quie - ro, quie - ro ver cuán - to a - mor a ti te

ca - be. Yo no ten - go pri - sa, yo me quie - ro dar el via - je. Em - pe - ce - mos

len - to, des - pués sal - va - je. Pa - si - to a pa - si - to, sua - ve sua - ve -

ci - to. Nos va - mos pe - gan - do po - qui - to a po - qui - to cuan - do tú me

be - sas con e - sa des - tre - za. Veo que e - res ma - li - cia con ___ de - li - ca -

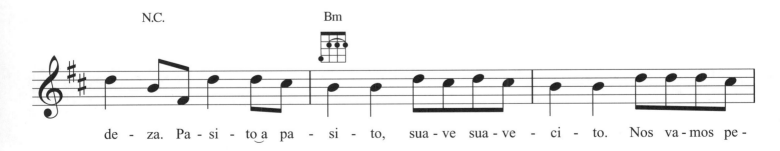

de - za. Pa - si - to a pa - si - to, sua - ve sua - ve - ci - to. Nos va - mos pe -

gan - do po - qui - to a po - qui - to. Y es que e - sa be - lle - za en un rom - pe - ca -

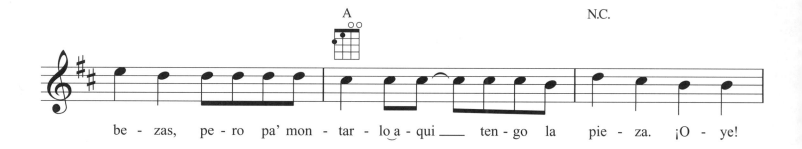

be - zas, pe - ro pa' mon - tar - lo a - qui ___ ten - go la pie - za. ¡O - ye!

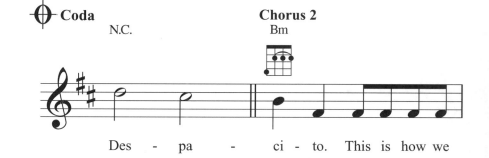

Coda

D.S. al Coda

Des - pa -

Chorus 2

Des - pa - ci - to. This is how we

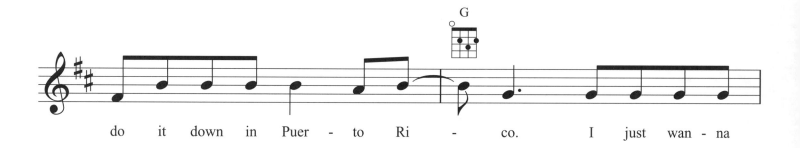

do it down in Puer - to Ri - co. I just wan - na

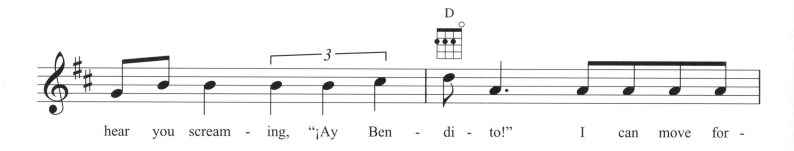

hear you scream - ing, "¡Ay Ben - di - to!" I can move for -

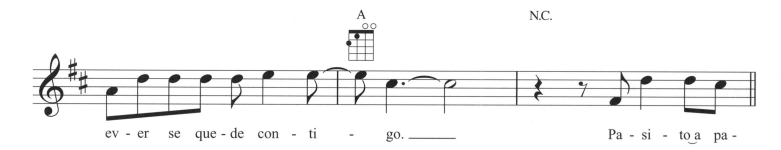

ev - er se que - de con - ti - go. ___ Pa - si - to a pa -

Outro-Bridge

si - to, sua-ve sua-ve - ci - to. Nos va-mos pe - gan-do po-qui-to a po-

qui - to.
Que le en - se - ñes a mi bo - ca, tus lu - ga - res fa - vo - ri -

- tos. _____ Pa - si - to a pa - si - to, sua - ve sua - ve -

ci - to. Nos va - mos pe - gan - do, po - qui - to a po -

qui - to.
Has - ta pro - vo - car tus gri - tos. Y que ol - vi - des ___ tu a - pe -

lli - do. Des - pa - ci - to.

Look What You Made Me Do

Words and Music by Taylor Swift, Jack Antonoff,
Richard Fairbrass, Fred Fairbrass and Rob Manzoli

First note

Verse
Urban Pop

N.C. (Am)

1. I don't like your lit - tle games, don't
2. I don't like your per - fect crime, how

like your tilt - ed stage. The
you laugh when you lie. You

1.
play of the fool. No, I don't like you.
mine. Is - n't cool. No, I

2.
don't like you.

Pre-Chorus

Am   Am7

But I got smart - er, I got hard - er in the nick of time.   Hon - ey, I rose up from the

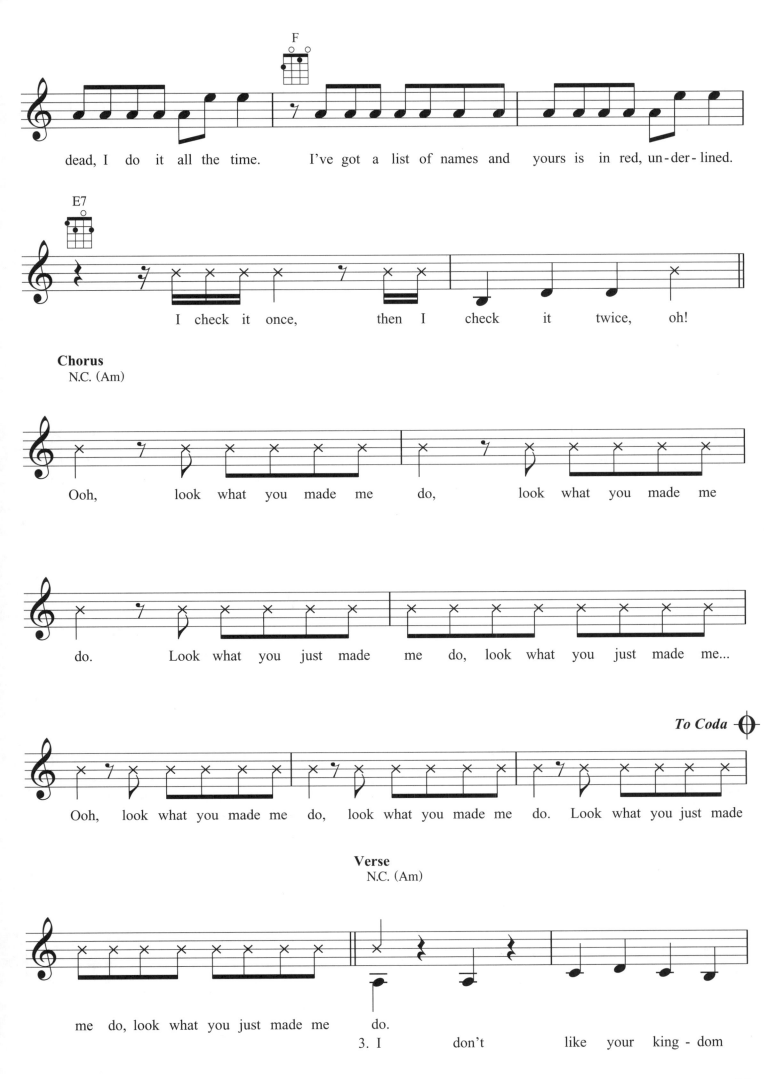

dead, I do it all the time. I've got a list of names and yours is in red, un-der-lined.

I check it once, then I check it twice, oh!

Chorus
N.C. (Am)

Ooh, look what you made me do, look what you made me

do. Look what you just made me do, look what you just made me...

To Coda

Ooh, look what you made me do, look what you made me do. Look what you just made

Verse
N.C. (Am)

me do, look what you just made me do. 3. I don't like your king-dom

keys, they once be - longed to me. You

asked me for a place to sleep, locked me out and threw a feast.

Pre-Chorus
N.C. (Am)

The world moves on, an - oth - er day, an - oth - er dra - ma, dra - ma.
And then the world moves on, but one thing's for sure:

1.

But not for me, not for me, all I think a - bout is kar - ma.
May - be I got mine, but you'll

2.

D.S. al Coda

all get yours.

Coda

me do, look what you just made me

Bridge

Am

F

do.
I don't trust no - bod - y and no - bod - y trusts me. I'll be the ac - tress

(Spoken:) "I'm sorry, the old Taylor can't come to the phone right now.

Why? *Oh,* *'cause she's dead!"*

Outro-Chorus

N.C. (Am)

Ooh, look what you made me do, look what you made me do. Look what you just made

1.

me do, look what you just made me...

2.

me do, look what you just made me

Am

do.   Look what you made me do,   look what you made me

Am7

do.   Look what you just made me do, look what you just made me...

F

Ooh,   look what you made me do,   look what you made me

E7   N.C.

do.   Look what you just made   me do, look what you just made me   do.

Evermore

from BEAUTY AND THE BEAST

Music by Alan Menken
Lyrics by Tim Rice

First note

Verse
Sturdy Ballad

1. I was the one ___ who had it all; ___

I was the mas - ter ___ of my fate.

I nev - er need - ed ___ an - y - bod - y in ___ my life;

I learned the truth ___ too late.

I'll nev - er shake a - way ___ the pain. ___

I close my eyes, __ but __ she's still there.

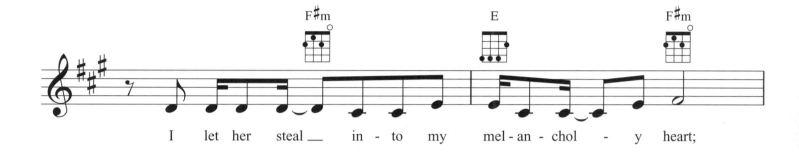

I let her steal __ in - to my mel - an - chol - y heart;

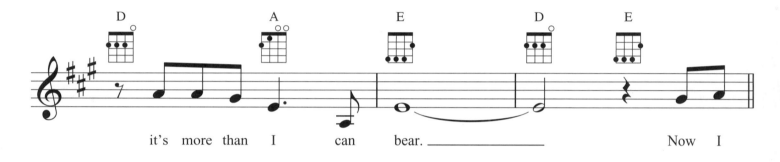

it's more than I can bear. _____ Now I

Chorus

know she'll nev - er leave me, e - ven as she runs a -

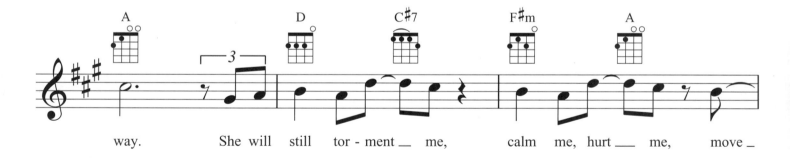

way. She will still tor - ment __ me, calm me, hurt __ me, move __

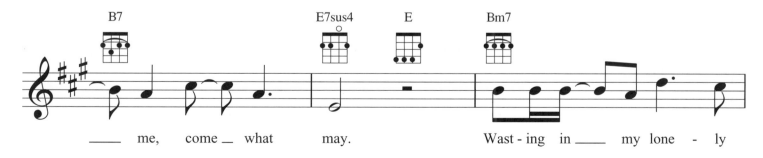

__ me, come __ what may. Wast - ing in __ my lone - ly

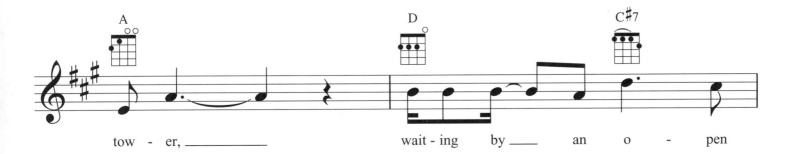

tow - er, _____ wait - ing by ___ an o - pen

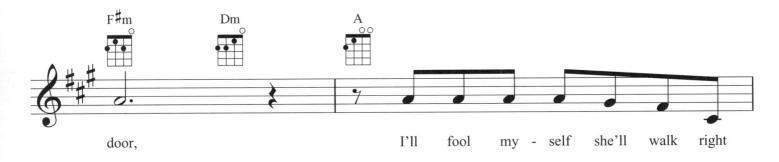

door, I'll fool my - self she'll walk right

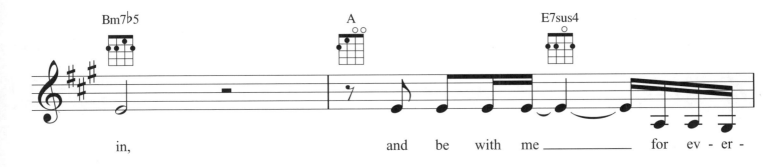

in, and be with me _____ for ev - er -

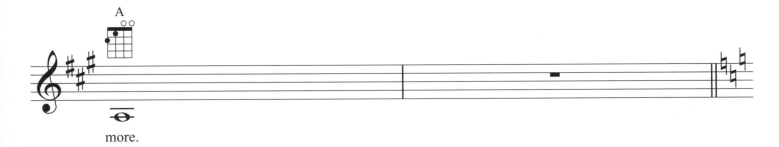

more.

Verse

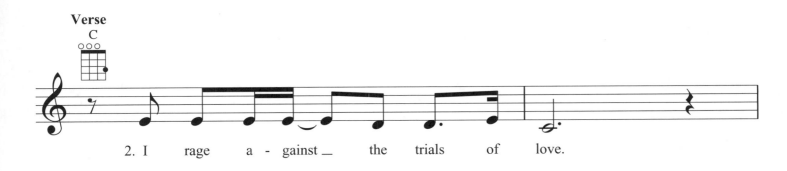

2. I rage a - gainst ___ the trials of love.

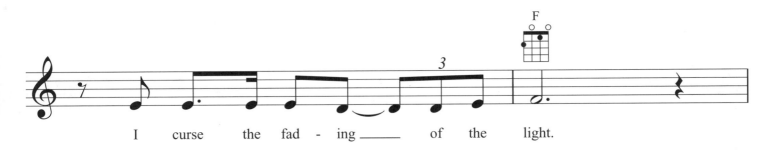

I curse the fad - ing _____ of the light.

Though she's al - read - y flown __ so far be - yond my reach,

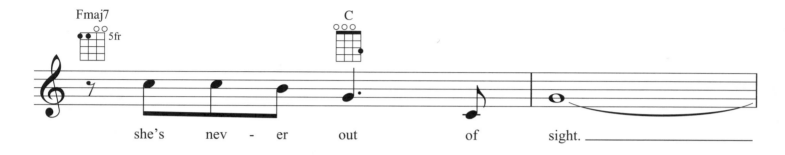

she's nev - er out of sight. _____

Chorus

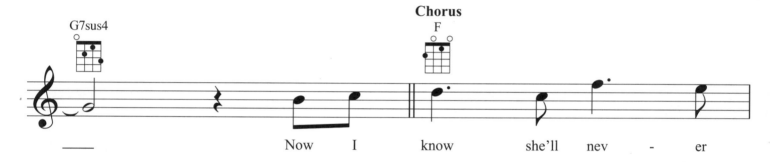

__ Now I know she'll nev - er

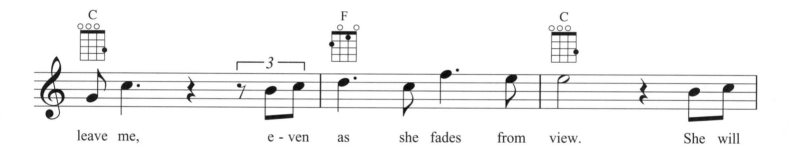

leave me, e - ven as she fades from view. She will

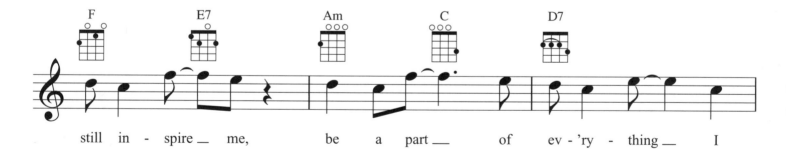

still in - spire __ me, be a part __ of ev - 'ry - thing __ I

do. Wast - ing in my lone - ly tow - er,

Human

Words and Music by Jamie Hartman and Rory Graham

Verse
Moderately slow groove

1. May - be I'm fool - ish, may - be I'm blind, ___
2. Take a look in the mir - ror and what do you see? ___
3. Don't ask my o - pin - ion, don't ask me to lie ___

___ think - ing I can see through ___ this and see what's be - hind. ___
___ Do you see it clear - er or are you de - ceived ___
___ then beg for ___ for - give - ness for mak - ing you cry, ___

___ Got no way to prove ___ it, so may - be I'm lyin'. ___ But I'm on - ly hu -
___ in what you be - lieved? ___ 'Cause I'm on - ly hu -
___ for mak - ing you cry. ___ 'Cause I'm on - ly hu -

- man af - ter all. ___ I'm on - ly hu - man af - ter all. ___ Don't put your blame on
- man af - ter all. ___ You're on - ly hu - man af - ter all. ___ Don't put the blame on
- man af - ter all. ___ I'm on - ly hu - man af - ter all. ___ Don't put your blame on

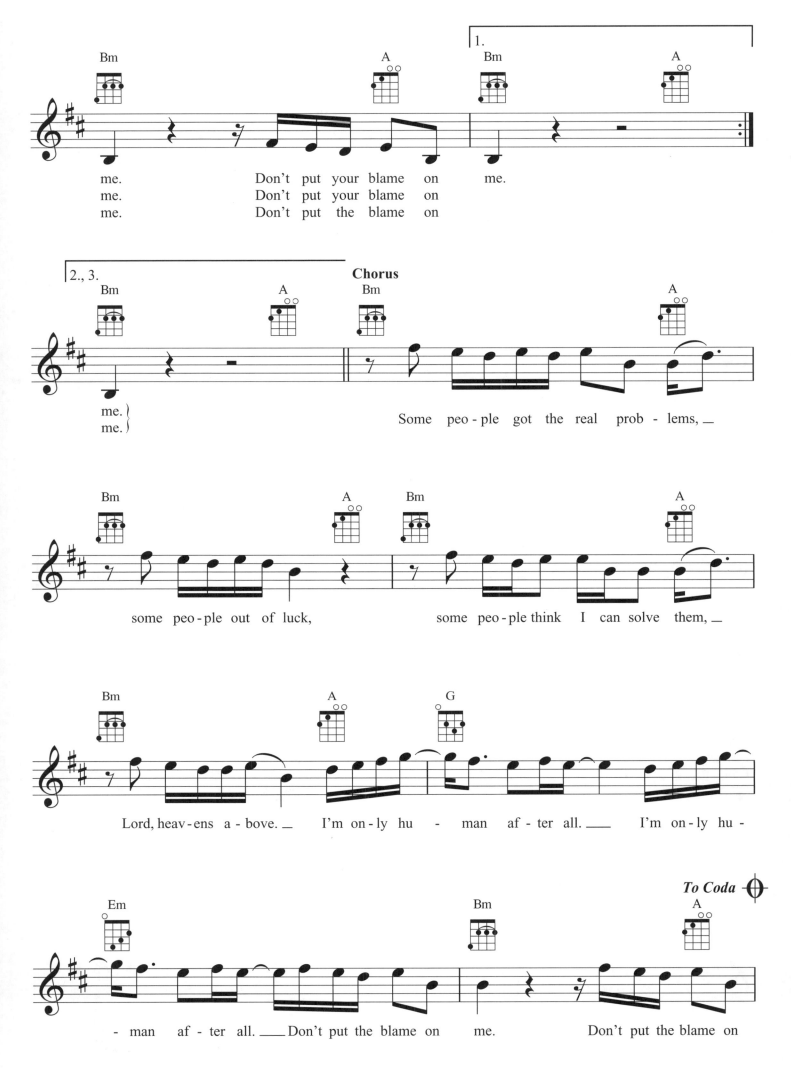

I Feel It Coming

Words and Music by Abel Tesfaye, Eric Chedeville, Guy-Manuel De Homem-Christo, Thomas Bangalter, Henry Walter and Martin McKinney

To Coda ⊕

in', babe.   I feel ___ it com - in',   I feel ___ it com -

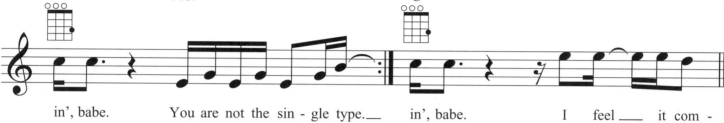

in', babe.   You are not the sin - gle type. ___ in', babe.   I feel ___ it com -

Chorus

in',   I feel ___ it com - in', babe.   I feel ___ it com -

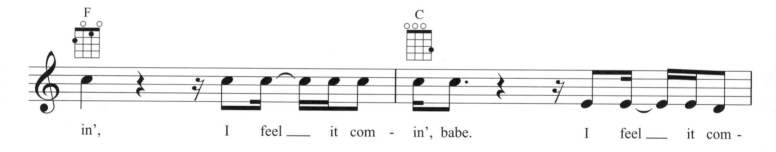

in',   I feel ___ it com - in', babe.   I feel ___ it com -

in',   I feel ___ it com - in', babe.   I feel ___ it com -

D.S. al Coda

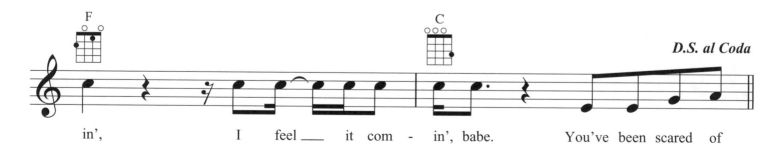

in',   I feel ___ it com - in', babe.   You've been scared of

Love on the Brain

Words and Music by Robyn Fenty, Joseph Angel and Frederik Ball

love me, ___ yeah. Just love me. ___ All you need to do is

love me, ___ yeah. Got me like, ah - ah - ah - ow.

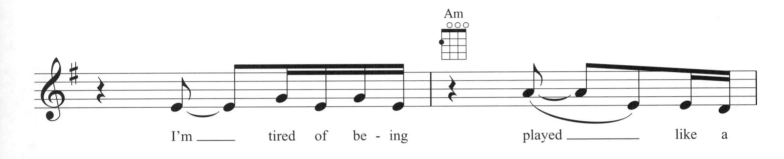

I'm ___ tired of be - ing played ___ like a

vi - o - lin. ___ What do I got ___ to do to get ___ in ___

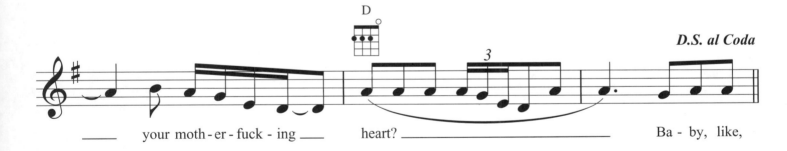

___ your moth - er - fuck - ing ___ heart? ___ Ba - by, like,

Coda

Must be love on ___ the brain. ___

Sign of the Times

Words and Music by Harry Styles, Jeffrey Bhasker, Alex Salibian,
Tyler Johnson, Mitch Rowland and Ryan Nasci

good — down here, but you ain't real - ly good. —
gain — some - where, some - where far a - way — from here.

Pre-Chorus

We nev - er learn; — we've been here be - fore.

Why are we al - ways stuck and run - ning from the bul - lets, the bul-

lets? We nev - er learn; — we been here be - fore.

Why are we al - ways stuck and run - ning from the bul - lets, the bul-

Chorus

lets? Just stop your cry - ing; it's a sign of the times. —

We got-ta get a - way __ from here.

We got-ta get a - way __ from here.

Just stop your cry -
Stop your cry - ing, ba -

- ing; it -'ll be al - right. _____
- by, it -'ll be al - right. _____

They told me that the

end __ is near. We got-ta get a - way __ from here.

Pre-Chorus

We nev-er learn; __ we've been here be-fore. Why are we al-ways stuck and

run-ning from the bul - lets, the bul - lets?

Bridge

We ___ don't talk e - nough; we ___ should
o - pen ___ up, be - fore ___ it's all too ___ much.
Will ___ we ev - er ___ learn? We've ___ been
here be - fore; ___ it's ___ just what we ___ know.

Chorus

Stop your cry - ing, ba - by; it's a sign of the times. _____

We got - ta get a - way. ___ We got to get a-

Slow Hands

**Words and Music by Niall Horan, John Henry Ryan, Alexander Izquierdo,
Ruth-Anne Cunningham, Tobias Jesso Jr. and Julian Bunetta**

sweat drip-pin' down our dirt-y laun - dry. No, no chance ___ that I'm

leav - in' here with - out you on me. I, I know, ___ yeah, I

al - read - y know that there ain't no stop - pin' your ___ plans and those

1.

Interlude

slow ___ hands. (Woo!) Slow hands.

2.

Bridge

Fin-ger-tips put-tin' on a show. Got me now and I can't say no.

Wan - na be with you all a - lone. Take ___ me home, take ___ me home. ___

Something Just Like This

Words and Music by Andrew Taggart, Chris Martin, Guy Berryman, Jonny Buckland and Will Champion

risk? I'm not look-ing for some-bod-y with some su-per-hu-man gifts, some su-per-he-ro, ___

To Coda ⊕

___ some fair-y-tale ___ bliss. Just some-thing I can turn to, some-bod-y I can

Chorus

kiss. I want some-thing just like ___ this. Do do do do do do do, ___ do do do do, ___

___ do do do do do do. Oh, I want some-thing just like ___

___ this. Do do do do do do do, ___ do do do do, ___ do do do do do do.

Oh, I want some-thing just like ___ this.

I want some-thing just like ____ this."

D.S. al Coda ⊕ **Coda**

2. I've been read-ing books of

miss. I want some-thing just like __

Chorus

____ this.

I want some-thing just like __

Oh, I want some-thing just like ____ this. Do do do do do do, ____

____ do do do do ____ do, ____ do do do do do do. Oh, I want some-thing just like __

____ this. Do do do do do do, ____ do do do do, ____ do do do do do do. ____

68

Outro

Where d'you wan-na go? __ How much you wan-na risk? I'm not look-ing for some -

bod-y with some su-per-hu-man gifts, some su-per-he-ro, ____ some fair-y-tale __

bliss. Just some-thing I can turn to, some-bod-y I can kiss. I want some-thing just like __

____ this.

Oh, I want some-thing just like ____ this.

Stay

Words and Music by Alessia Caracciolo, Anders Froen, Jonnali Parmenius, Sarah Aarons, Anton Zaslavski and Linus Wiklund

1. Wait-ing for the time to pass you by, _____
2. Won't ad-mit what I al-read-y know, _____ I've

hope the winds of change will change your mind. _____
nev-er been the best at let-ting go. _____

I could give a thou-sand rea-sons why. _____ And I know
I don't wan-na spend the night a-lone. _____ Guess I need _____

_____ you, and you've got _____ to
_____ you, and I need _____ to _____

Pre-Chorus

make it on your own, but we don't have to grow up, we can stay for-ev-er young.
make it on my own, but I don't wan-na grow up, we can stay for-ev-er young.

Liv-ing on my so-fa, drink-ing rum and co-la un-der-neath the ris-ing sun.
Liv-ing on my so-fa, drink-ing rum and co-la un-der-neath the ris-ing sun.

I could give a thou-sand rea-sons why ___ but you're go-
I could give a mil-lion rea-sons why ___ but I'm go-

- ing, and you know ___ that ___) all you have to do is
- ing, and you know ___ that ___)

𝄋 Chorus

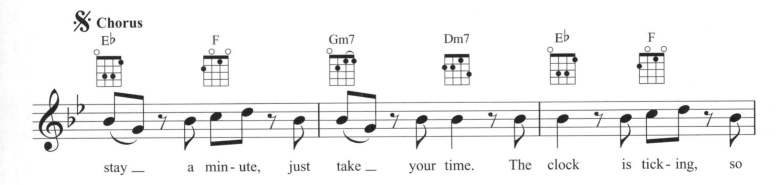

stay ___ a min-ute, just take ___ your time. The clock is tick-ing, so

stay. ___ All you have to do is wait ___ a sec-ond, your

To Coda ⊕

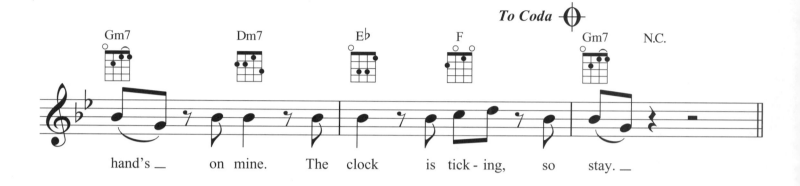

hand's ___ on mine. The clock is tick-ing, so stay. ___

Interlude

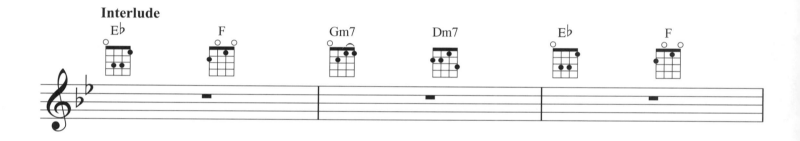

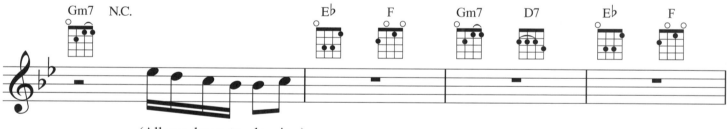

(All you have to do is...)

1.   2.

Bridge

All you have to do is stay. ___   stay. ___

All you have to do is stay, _____

so stay. ___

D.S. al Coda

All you have to do is

⊕ **Coda**

stay. ___ All you have to do is

Outro

stay. ___ (Mmm, _____ mmm, _____

mmm, _____ mmm.) _____

That's What I Like

Words and Music by Bruno Mars, Philip Lawrence, James Fauntleroy, Ray Charles McCullough II, Christopher Brody Brown, Jeremy Reeves, Jonathan Yip and Ray Romulus

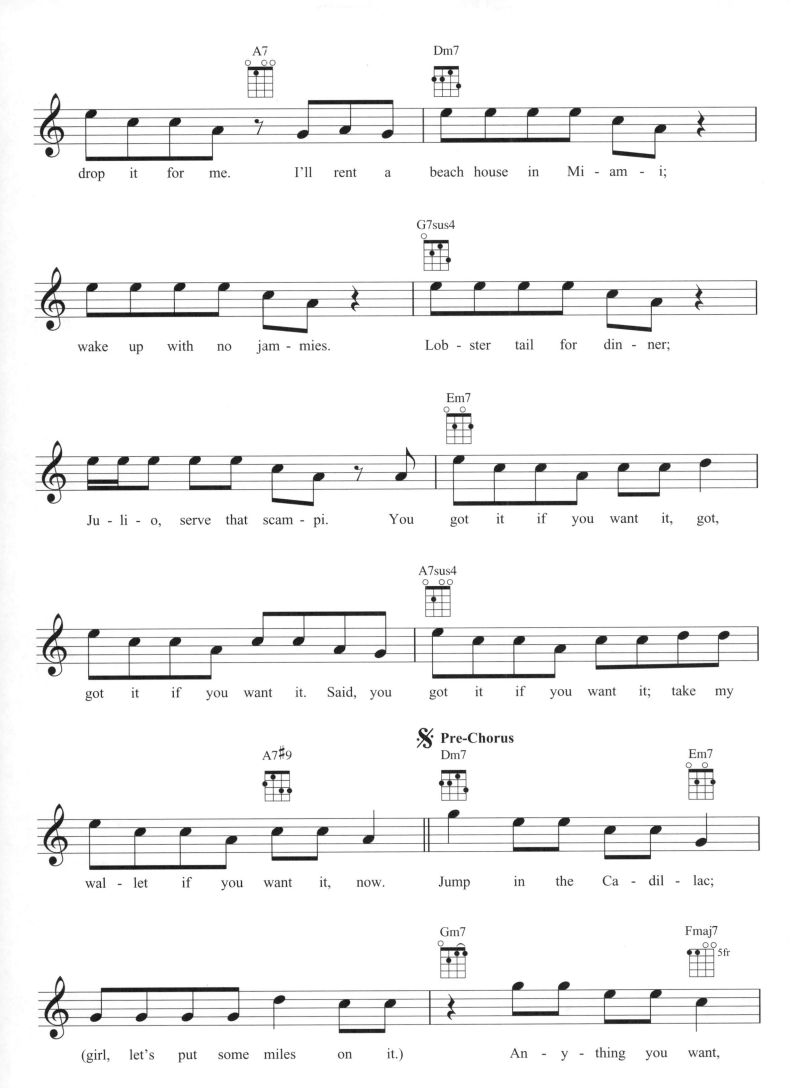

drop it for me.   I'll rent a   beach house in   Mi - am - i;

wake   up   with   no   jam - mies.   Lob - ster   tail   for   din - ner;

Ju - li - o,   serve   that   scam - pi.   You   got   it   if   you   want   it,   got,

got   it   if   you   want   it.   Said,   you   got   it   if   you   want   it;   take   my

§ Pre-Chorus

wal - let   if   you   want   it,   now.   Jump   in   the   Ca - dil - lac;

(girl,   let's   put   some   miles   on   it.)   An - y - thing   you   want,

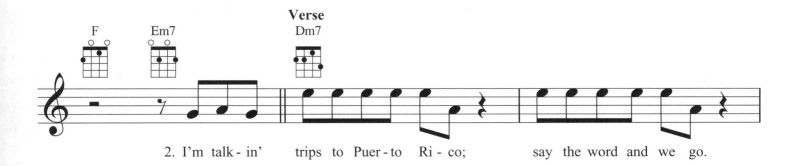

Verse

2. I'm talk-in' trips to Puer-to Ri-co; say the word and we go.

You can be my freek-a; girl, I'll be a flee-ko, *ma - ma -*

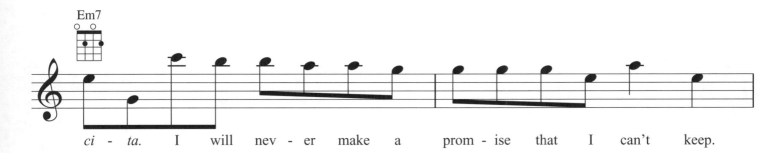

ci - ta. I will nev - er make a prom - ise that I can't keep.

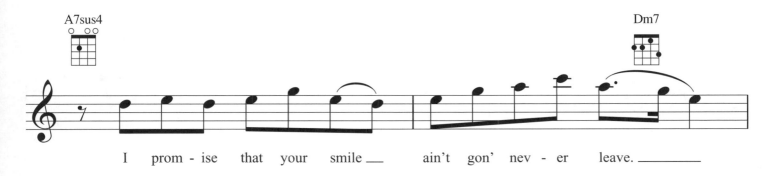

I prom - ise that your smile ___ ain't gon' nev - er leave. ___

Shop - ping sprees in Par - is; ev - 'ry-thing twen - ty - four kar - ats.

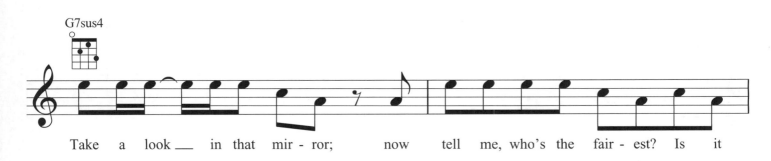

Take a look ___ in that mir - ror; now tell me, who's the fair - est? Is it

you? (Is it you?) Is it me? (Is it me?) Say it's us, (say it's us,) and I'll a-

D.S. al Coda

Coda

gree, _____ ba - by.

You say you want a

Bridge

good _____ time, _____ well, here I am, ba - by,

here I am, ba - by. (Talk to me, talk to me, talk to me, tell me what's

on your __ mind.) _____ If you want it,

What's on your mind? __

girl, come and get it; ____ all this is here _____ for you.

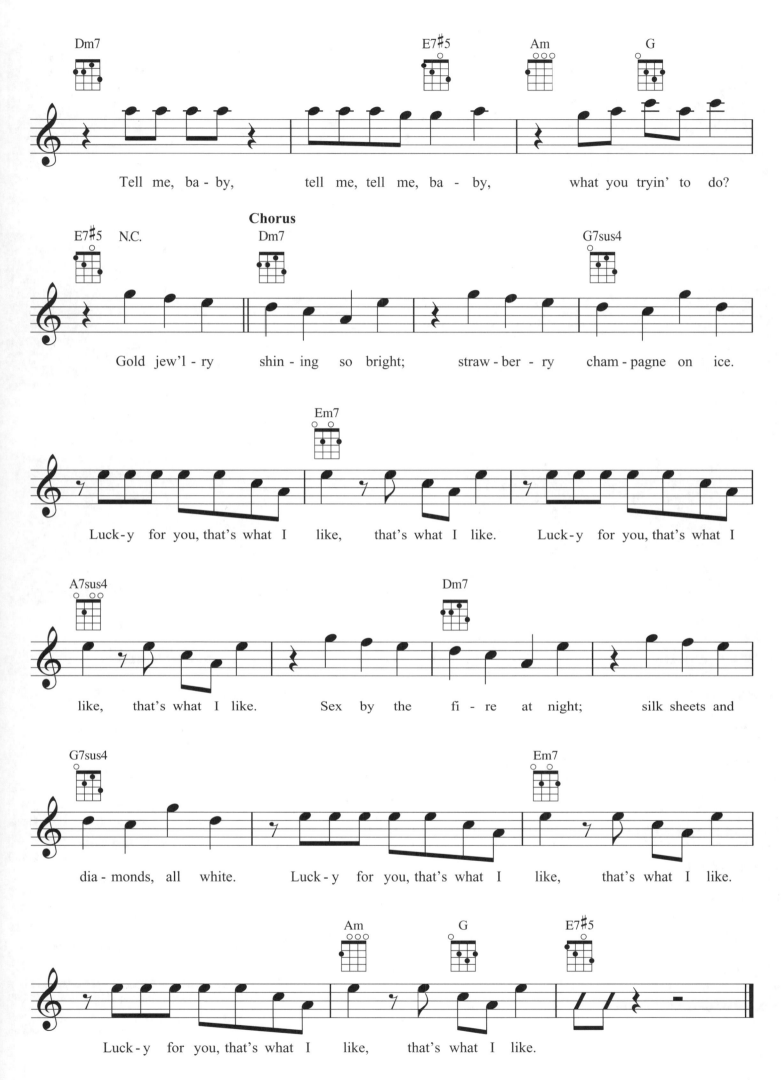

Hal•Leonard® UKULELE PLAY-ALONG

AUDIO ACCESS INCLUDED

Now you can play your favorite songs on your uke with great-sounding backing tracks to help you sound like a bona fide pro! The audio also features playback tools so you can adjust the tempo without changing the pitch and loop challenging parts.

Prices, contents, and availability subject to change without notice.

HAL•LEONARD®
www.halleonard.com

0817